Christmas 1993

Dear Anne,

You are always there for me.

Love,

Dianna

FRIENDS

FRIENDS

An Illustrated Treasury of Friendship

Compiled by Michelle Lovric

COURAGE BOOKS

an imprint of
RUNNING PRESS
Philadelphia, Pennsylvania

Copyright © 1993 by Royle Publications Limited.
　　　Royle House
　　　Wenlock Road
　　　London N1 7ST
　　　England
Concept developed by Michelle Lovric
　　　53 Shelton Street
　　　Covent Garden
　　　London WC2H 9HE
　　　England

Canadian representatives: General Publishing Co., Ltd., 30 Lesmill Road, Don Mills, Ontario M3B 2T6.

9 8 7 6 5 4 3 2 1
Digit on the right indicates the number of this printing.

Library of Congress Cataloging-in-Publication Number 92–54933
ISBN 1–56138–273–6
Cover design by Toby Schmidt
Cover illustration by William Marshall Brown
Interior design by Christian Benton
Text edited by Melissa Stein
Typography by Richard Conklin

Published by Courage Books, an imprint of
Running Press Book Publishers
125 South Twenty-second Street
Philadelphia, Pennsylvania 19103

The publishers gratefuly acknowledge the permission of the following to reproduce copyrighted material in this book:
p. 21: From "Stopping at a Friend's Farm" by Meng Hao-Jan, translated by Daniel Bryant, from *Sunflower Splendour*, published by the Indiana University Press. Originally published by Doubleday, Anchor Books. Copyright © 1975 Wu-Chi Lu and Irving Lao.
p. 28: From "Lies about Love," from *The Complete Poems of D.H. Lawrence*, published by Viking Penguin, a division of Penguin Books of U.S.A. Inc. Copyright © 1964, 1971 by Angelo Ravagli and C.M. Weckley, Executors of the estate of Frieda Lawrence Ravagli.

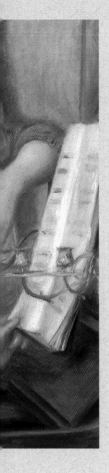

THE ORIGINS OF FRIENDSHIP ARE A CELEBRATED MYSTERY. FRIENDSHIP BLESSES AND REFRESHES; ITS GIFTS ARE LAUGHTER, UNDERSTANDING, AND STRENGTH. IT IS A RELATIONSHIP THAT EXISTS APART FROM THE CLAIMS OF FAMILY AND LOVERS.

IN CHOOSING OUR FRIENDS, WE MAKE IMPORTANT DECISIONS ABOUT WHO WE ARE. OUR FRIENDS DO NOT OWE US THEIR LOVE OR APPROVAL—THESE WE MUST EARN, AND IN DOING SO, WE BECOME VULNERABLE. BUT ONCE ESTABLISHED, FRIENDSHIP IS A SIMPLE PLEASURE, A PLACE WHERE WE CAN BE OURSELVES WITHOUT WEIGHING OUR WORDS OR WATCHING OUR MANNERS.

ART DELIGHTS IN FRIENDSHIP, AND CAN DEMONSTRATE THE WAY IN WHICH COMPANIONSHIP TRULY ALTERS THE LANDSCAPE FOR US. FRIENDSHIP'S IMAGES ARE FULL OF COLOR AND WARMTH, RICH WITH VIBRANT DETAIL, AND ALIVE WITH FEELING.

WHAT IS A FRIEND?
A SINGLE SOUL DWELLING
IN TWO BODIES.

Aristotle (384–322 B.C.)
Greek philosopher

Friends

do not

live in

harmony

merely,

as some say,

but in melody.

HENRY DAVID THOREAU (1817–1862)
AMERICAN WRITER

Oh, the comfort, the inexpressible comfort
of feeling safe with a person;
having neither to weigh thoughts nor
measure words,
but pour them out, just as they are,
chaff and grain together,
Knowing that a faithful hand will take and
sift them,
keep what is worth keeping,
And then with the breath of kindness, blow
the rest away.

DINAH MARIA MULOCK CRAIK (1826–1887)
ENGLISH WRITER

*I*ALWAYS FELT THAT THE GREAT

HIGH PRIVILEGE, RELIEF AND

COMFORT OF FRIENDSHIP WAS THAT

ONE HAD TO EXPLAIN NOTHING.

Katherine Mansfield (1888–1923)
English writer

A friend is a second self; another I.

ZENO (C. 355 B.C.)
GREEK PHILOSOPHER

$\mathcal{T}$ell me what company thou keepest,

and I'll tell thee what thou art.

MIGUEL DE CERVANTES (1547–1616)
SPANISH NOVELIST

FRIENDSHIP IS A

SHELTERING

TREE.

Samuel Taylor Coleridge (1772–1834)
English poet

True friendship is a plant of slow growth.

GEORGE WASHINGTON (1732–1799)
FIRST PRESIDENT OF THE UNITED STATES

THE BIRD A NEST,

THE SPIDER A WEB,

MAN FRIENDSHIP.

William Blake (1757–1827)
English poet and painter

Fate chooses your relations,
you choose your friends.

JACQUES DELILLE (1738–1813)
FRENCH ABBE AND POET

We cannot tell the precise moment

when friendship is formed. As in

filling a vessel drop by drop, there

is at last a drop which makes it

run over; so in a series of

kindnesses there is at last one

which makes the heart run over.

JAMES BOSWELL (1740–1795)
ENGLISH WRITER

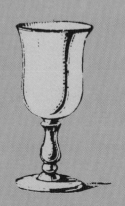

TWO MAY TALK TOGETHER UNDER THE SAME ROOF FOR MANY YEARS, YET NEVER REALLY MEET; AND TWO OTHERS AT FIRST SPEECH ARE OLD FRIENDS.

Mary Catherwood (1847–1901)
American writer

If there were only two men in the world,

how would they get on?

They would help one another,

harm one another,

flatter one another,

slander one another,

fight one another,

make it up;

they could neither live together

nor do without one another.

VOLTAIRE (FRANCOIS–JEAN AROUET) (1694–1778)
FRENCH WRITER AND PHILOSOPHER

A new person is to me always a great

event and hinders me from sleep.

RALPH WALDO EMERSON (1803–1882)
AMERICAN WRITER

YES'M, OLD FRIENDS IS

ALWAYS BEST,

'LESS YOU CAN CATCH

A NEW ONE THAT'S

FIT TO MAKE

AN OLD ONE OUT OF.

Sarah Orne Jewett (1849–1909)
American writer

My old friend prepares chicken and millet,

And invites me to visit his home in the fields.

Green trees enclose the country village,

Blue hills slope upward from the outskirts,

Opening the window, we face fields and garden,

Lifting our cups, talk of mulberry and hemp.

Wait till the Autumn Festival comes again,

I will return in time for the blooming of the chrysanthemums.

MENG HAO-JAN (689–740)
CHINESE POET

'WILL YOU BE MY FRIEND, MY FRIEND OF FRIENDS, BEYOND EVERY ONE, EVERYTHING, FOREVER AND FOREVER?'

Henry James (1843–1916)
American writer

Separateness is sweet but connection with someone outside yourself is surely sweeter.

JUDITH VIORST, B. 1931
AMERICAN WRITER

HOW I LIKE TO BE LIKED, AND WHAT I DO TO BE LIKED!

Charles Lamb (1775–1834)
English writer

I had three chairs in my house;

one for solitude,

two for friendship,

three for society.

Henry David Thoreau (1817–1862)
American writer

I want someone to laugh with me,

someone to be grave with me,

someone to please me and help my

discrimination with his or her own remark,

and at times, no doubt, to admire

my acuteness and penetration.

ROBERT BURNS (1759–1796)
SCOTTISH POET

Assume that we are friends. Assume

A common taste for old costume,

Old pictures,–books. Then dream us sitting,–

Us two,–in some soft-lighted room....

We, with our faces toward the fire,

Finished the feast not full but fitting,

Watch the light-leaping flames aspire.

HENRY AUSTIN DOBSON (1840–1921)
ENGLISH WRITER

. . . A TIME COMES IN EVERY HUMAN

FRIENDSHIP WHEN YOU MUST GO

DOWN INTO THE DEPTHS OF YOURSELF,

AND LAY BARE WHAT IS THERE TO YOUR

FRIEND, AND WAIT IN FEAR FOR HIS

ANSWER.

Thomas Hughes (1822–1896)
English jurist, reformer and writer

The love I feel for my friend, this year,

is different from the love I felt last year.

If it were not so, it would be a lie.

Yet we re-iterate love! love!

as if it were a coin with a fixed value

instead of a flower that dies, and opens a different bud.

D.H. LAWRENCE (1885–1930)
ENGLISH NOVELIST

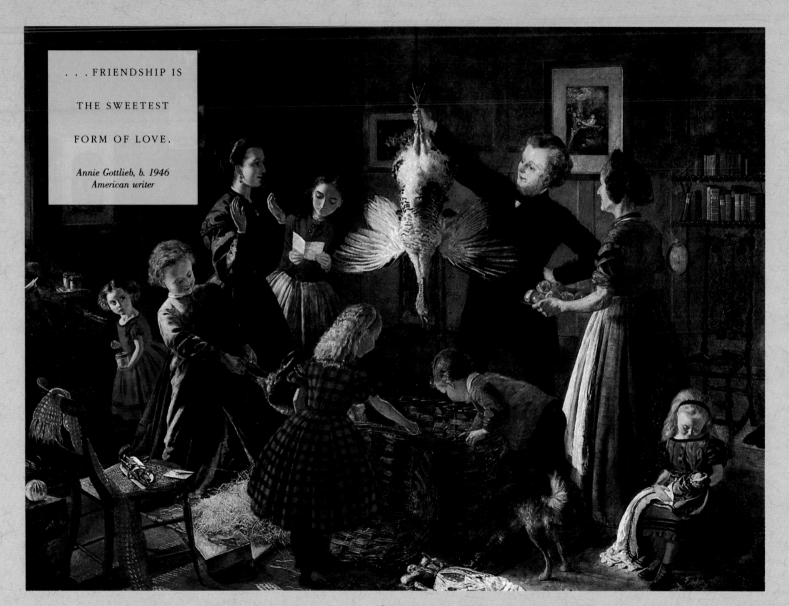

. . . FRIENDSHIP IS

THE SWEETEST

FORM OF LOVE.

Annie Gottlieb, b. 1946
American writer

Friendship, as some sage poet sings,

Is chastened Love, deprived of wings,

Without all wish or power to wander,

Less volatile, but not less tender.

CHARLOTTE SMITH (1749–1806)
ENGLISH WRITER

I wish that friendship should have feet,
as well as eyes and eloquence.
It must plant itself on the ground,
before it walks over the moon.

RALPH WALDO EMERSON (1803–1882)
AMERICAN WRITER

Love is blind; friendship closes its eyes.

PROVERB

FRIENDSHIP IS A MIRACLE

BY WHICH A PERSON

CONSENTS TO VIEW

FROM A CERTAIN DISTANCE,

AND WITHOUT COMING

ANY NEARER,

THE VERY BEING

WHO IS NECESSARY

TO HIM AS FOOD.

Simone Weil (1909–1943)
French philosopher

Nothing makes the earth
seem so spacious
as to have friends
at a distance;
they make
the latitudes
and longitudes.

HENRY DAVID THOREAU (1817–1862)
AMERICAN WRITER

Sir, more than kisses, letters mingle souls;

For, thus absent friends speak.

John Donne (1572–1631)
English poet and cleric

When a person that one loves

is in the world and alive and

well . . . then to miss them is

only a new flavor, a salt

sharpness in experience.

Winifred Holtby (1898–1935)
English writer

Friends depart, and memory takes them

To her caverns, pure and deep.

THOMAS HAYNES BAYLY (1797–1839)
BRITISH WRITER

When to the sessions of sweet silent thought,

I summon up remembrance of things past,

I sigh the lack of many a thing I sought,

And with old woes new wail my dear time's waste:

Then can I drown an eye, unus'd to flow,

For precious friends hid in death's dateless night,

And weep afresh love's long since cancell'd woe,

And moan th'expense of many a vanish'd sight...

But if the while I think on thee, dear friend,

All losses are restor'd and sorrows end.

William Shakespeare (1564–1616)
English dramatist

There is no wilderness like a life
without friends; friendship
multiplies blessing and minimises
misfortunes; it is a unique remedy
against adversity, and it soothes
the soul.

BALTASAR GRACIAN (1601–1658)
SPANISH WRITER

FRIENDSHIP IS CERTAINLY THE FINEST BALM FOR THE PANGS OF DISAPPOINTED LOVE.

Jane Austen (1775–1817)
English writer

It is not so much
our friends' help
that helps us
as the confident
knowledge that they
will help us.

EPICURUS (341–270 B.C.)
GREEK PHILOSOPHER

*T*he only way to have a friend is to be one.

RALPH WALDO EMERSON (1803–1882)
AMERICAN WRITER

WHEN MY FRIENDS LACK AN EYE,

I LOOK AT THEM IN PROFILE.

Joseph Joubert (1754–1824)
French essayist and moralist

We all love best not those who offend us least, nor those who have done most for us, but those who make it most easy for us to forgive them.

SAMUEL BUTLER (1612–1680)
ENGLISH POET

We give and take

With no line in between.

MARGE PIERCY, B. 1936
AMERICAN POET

REINFORCE

THE STITCH

THAT TIES US,

AND I WILL

DO THE SAME

FOR YOU.

Doris Schwerin, b. 1922
American writer

Don't walk before me, I may not follow,

Don't walk behind me, I may not lead,

Just walk beside me, and be my friend.

ALBERT CAMUS (1913–1960)
FRENCH WRITER

Anything,

everything,

little or big

becomes an adventure

when the right

person shares it.

KATHLEEN NORRIS (1880–1966)
AMERICAN WRITER

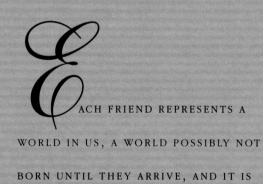

EACH FRIEND REPRESENTS A

WORLD IN US, A WORLD POSSIBLY NOT

BORN UNTIL THEY ARRIVE, AND IT IS

ONLY BY THIS MEETING THAT A NEW

WORLD IS BORN.

Anaïs Nin (1903–1977)
French-born American writer

ILLUSTRATION ACKNOWLEDGMENTS

COVER: *On the Beach,* William Marshall Brown
(Fine Art Photographic Library Limited)

p. 1 [detail]: *Yuletide in Canada,* artist unknown

pp. 4–5 [detail]: *The Sledge Ride,* L. S. Cabaillot
(Fine Art Photographic Library Limited)

pp. 6–7 [detail]: *Jeune Filles au Piano,* Pierre Auguste Renoir
(Musee d'Orsay, Paris)

p. 9: *On the Beach,* William Marshall Brown
(Fine Art Photographic Library Limited)

p. 10: *The Toy Boat,* Frantz Charlet
(MacConnal–Mason Gallery, St. James's, London SW1)

pp. 12–13: *The Little Flower Sellers,* Alexei A. Harlamoff
(MacConnal–Mason Gallery, St. James's, London SW1)

pp. 14–15 [detail]: *The Bayswater Omnibus,* George William Joy
(Museum of London)

p. 17: *A Toast to the Bride,* Walter Dendy Sadler
(MacConnal–Mason Gallery, St. James's, London SW1)

p. 18: *Dimanche a Bellvue,* Gabriel Amable de la Foulhouze
(Fine Art Photographic Library Limited)